Surviving the Distance

Surviving the Distance

The Do's, the Don'ts, and the
Definitely's of Surviving a Long
Distance Relationship

Shauna and Taurean Curry

One Mic Publishing

Surviving The Distance: The Do's, the Don'ts and the Definitely's of Surviving a Long Distance Relationship

Shauna and Taurean Curry

My Open Letter

Dear Reader,

For those of you who may think this journey was easy for us, the truth is, it definitely was not. I'll be the first to say our relationship has been far from perfect, but as we look back, we find a new appreciation for the imperfection. As you will soon read in the upcoming chapter, Shauna and I dated on and off for some time, took an extended break (and I mean EXTENDED), and somehow came back to each other despite being separated by many state lines. If I'm being honest during the time we were "on and off" and even a year or two when we got back together, I was VERY immature (my wife would probably add a few extra "very's" in there). It isn't the easiest thing to admit, but honestly speaking it took me some time to realize how great of a woman I had in front of me.

It's almost as if it just hit me one day randomly during a conversation. An "aha moment" if you will, where I literally had to question myself and say, "Wait a second, what am I doing? She is everything I want in a life partner, wife, and soulmate. What exactly am I waiting for?" I literally wrote a dissertation in my head at that moment, summarizing how important she was to me. The next step I needed to take became very clear.

To this day there are times when I look back and ask myself how did we make it through this? During times of reflection, I'm reminded it involved a lot of patience, understanding, forgiveness, faith, communication, and love. Out of it all, we experienced a tremendous amount of growth and closeness in our relationship. An incredible amount of maturation and development that we otherwise aren't sure we could have attained any other way. Simply stated, the distance was the best thing that happened for our relationship.

And to my wife; I can go on and on about the characteristics and qualities I adore about you, but this would turn into a romantic novel very quickly. It's hard to pinpoint one thing specifically, but your willingness to expose your vulnerabilities has always struck a chord with me. You see, through our journey together I've realized the key to making a deep connection is vulnerability. It took me some time to truly comprehend this, but vulnerability is the act that allows us as human beings to connect on a stronger level and a stronger connection leads to true intimacy. Not physical intimacy, but rather emotional intimacy. An emotional intimacy that I was missing before you showed up in my life. Thank you for your patience, Thank you for your Trust, and Thank You for being by my side through thick and thin.

Taurean

Table of Contents

Preface: The Back Story

This Love saga started 13 years ago when Taurean and I both lived in Houston, the greatest city on earth (took a second to laugh as I pictured the face of all the non-Houstonians as I typed this). We met when we were working at the same company and by my account, I was feeling myself and made the first move. By his account, he used his witty charm to get me to say yes to a first date. For this portion of our love story, we will not get into all the details of the beginning of our relationship (that would be a 2nd book and more of a dramatic, tragedy, thriller-romance novel). But we would like to express to our readers that it was not ALL rainbows and unicorns right from the very beginning. Actually, we took a long break from each other after our first two years of dating. Throughout the years following our breakup, we randomly would reconnect or communicate, but just could not figure it out. As life would have it, we both had to go through a series of different relationships before the universe reconnected us in 2014.

This time around though it was different. I was still in Houston but Taurean was now living in California working in Silicon Valley, 27 hours and 1,800 miles away. Along with the obstacle of distance, there was the history of a failed relationship that did not end well the first time. We went into our new relationship with a lot of old perceptions and ideologies about each other and our past. But, despite some major distance and history, we were very sure about one thing. We knew it was a reason we came back to each other and did not want to waste any more time not exploring how we could figure things out to make our relationship work. We never seriously had the intention of being in a long-distance relationship; it just kind of transpired. As time passed we began to slowly fall in love with each other to the point where we felt there was no other choice but to continue to move forward despite the major obstacle in front of us. Hence the start of our LDR (Long Distance Relationship), which I always referred to as my "California Love" in 2014. So here we are 6 Years later (married for 2), parents of 4 amazing young men, and working on a beautiful baby girl to complete our tribe. But despite our "happy ending", we DEFINITELY would have loved to have the survival tips we are going to share with you in the upcoming chapters a heck of a lot earlier!

In this book, we will share our experiences and obstacles and how we overcame and survived the struggles associated with long-distance relationships. With each passing chapter, we will share survival tips, the **Do's**, the **Don'ts**, and the **Definitely's**, of LDR'S. It is our hope that other couples going through a similar stage within their relationship can use this as a valuable resource.

Chapter One: How Common are LDR's

It was not until we started writing this book that we realized that LDRs are very common. According to longdistancerelationshps.net 14 to 15 million people consider themselves in a long-distance relationship. 3.75 million married couples are in an LDR and 75% of all engaged couples have been (at some point) in a long-distance relationship.

Although an LDR isn't ideal, we found out that there are some real advantages that come with the territory. For instance, did you know there were some amazing benefits that come with frequently flying!? Southwest Airlines was our best friend and for 3 years we qualified for their Companion Pass, which meant anywhere one of us flew the other could fly too for FREE! Not to mention the improved communication skills, a relationship based on more than just sex, and the Awesome story you are creating to tell your grandchildren (wink, wink).

Other studies point out long-distance relationships may be just as stable or even more stable in some cases than assumed but only if certain conditions are met. One study in particular (Dargie et al, 2015) examined the relationships of 1,142 couples. Surprisingly, the research found no evidence that LDRs are at all different when it comes to things such as intimacy, communication, relationship satisfaction, commitment, and sexual communication or satisfaction.

Chapter Two: Communication is Key

So, like any other relationship, LDR or not, there's always something magical about being in love and excited to spend every moment you can with your significant other. When you are in an LDR, the excitement seems even more elevated because of the limited time that you actually spend together in person. When Taurean and I got back together, the very first time I flew out to see him it was one of the best times we had ever spent together. I was so excited to get on the plane and felt butterflies of anticipation the entire flight. I felt like a giggly schoolgirl when he picked me up from the airport. I was so impressed that he took the time to plan our long weekend together. Every day was date night, we stayed up all night talking, laughing, and "enjoying" each other's company and when the time came for me to leave 3 days later, (no exaggeration) I cried. It was love at first sight, over and over again, every time we saw each other for an entire 12 months. Then, the 13th month came and all of sudden, the excitement to jump on a plane after a long week of work was not as enticing. I was no longer that giggly schoolgirl. I had morphed into a middle-aged woman, with kids, a job, bills, and very little time to be traipsing back and forth to California every other month. That night, when he picked me up from the airport (late, I might add), I was exhausted from a very long day at work. The 5-hour flight I had just arrived on was delayed which made my travel time way longer than expected. It was a super bumpy flight and kept me from falling to sleep, which is by the way completely necessary due to my major flight anxiety. Not to mention I was still irritated by the argument we had 2 days before about him not answering the phone. Most importantly, I was irritated because I was still waiting for a definite answer on "Who was going to move to the other city?" My favorite phrase had turned from, "I can't wait until we can be in the same city" to, "We need to figure out which one of us is moving, cause I'm not doing this long-distance crap for forever". Back then I was quickly becoming "over it". Looking back now, I may or may not have been a tad bit of a drama queen. Thankfully, with a whole lot of patience, tons of passion, blind faith, and an abundance of pure stubbornness we got to the point where we eventually figured it out.

Survival Tip #1: Know how your partner Communicates their love for you, and know-how you receive it

Ok so, Lord knows it took us a long time to figure out how to effectively communicate with each other, and it was not until I was introduced to a book by the name of the 5 LOVE LANGUAGES, that I realized we had definitely been doing it all wrong. If I could give my younger self any advice, it would be to pick up this book 15 years ago. You will hear us talk about communication a lot in this book because it truly is the foundation of any lasting relationship. In an LDR, it is almost singularly the one thing that can make or break you and your partner. The 5 love languages not only taught us more on how to effectively communicate with each other but also how to truly UNDERSTAND how each of us received and interpreted words, and actions.

Now, in our case, it took my now-husband 1 year to read and take the love language quiz after I asked him to. But as the saying goes, better late than never.

What is a Love Language, you may ask? A love Language is how a person innately expresses and experiences love and there are 5 of them. Words of Affirmation, Quality Time, Physical Touch, Acts of Service, and Gifts. After reading, we had a better understanding of how each of us felt loved and understood. It made our relationship 100% better and we no longer wasted words or actions on each other that weren't conducive to our growth as a couple. After taking the quiz, I realized my number 1 Love Language was Physical Touch and his was Quality

Time. We were on 2 separate sides of the spectrum! It was a Major " Ahh ha" moment for us.

Taking the Five Love Language assessment to identify our languages made everything make sense when I looked back on the things that caused us to have so much tension. I remember one huge argument we had about hand-holding. We were walking around the mall and I went to hold Taurean's hand, and he switched his phone from the hand he was holding it with to the hand I was trying to hold! Being that it was the 5th time he did that, I went off! I was like, "Dude I'm flying across the country to be with you, and you can't even hold my hand?" And it quickly turned into, "What? Are you ashamed of me? Which escalated even further to, "You got another girlfriend in California or something that you don't want to bump into holding my hand in this mall?" (OH, where our crazy little minds will go, when we let it). I now understand, Taurean's reaction to hand-holding didn't have anything to do with what he did or did not think of me but everything to do with the way he received and understood love. When a person has a particular love language it's easy for them to believe that everyone else has the exact same love language. So, when they show love, they give it HOW THEY WANT TO RECEIVE IT. In our relationship physical touch was nowhere on Taureans radar, he felt the most love when I gave him my undivided attention. So, when I wanted to cuddle and all he wanted to do was sit on the couch a foot apart, I was a little annoyed and hurt that he didn't love me enough. And when I was scrolling on my phone while he was talking about a podcast he listened to or something he was interested in, not looking him in the eyes and giving one-sentence answers, he became irritated and would completely shut down. It took some time to realize the little things with respect to the way we responded and communicated with each other were what was either breathing life into our relationship or sucking the air right out of it. It was when we both became intentional about showing love the way each other could openly receive and understand it, that we really began to develop a deeper connection and love for one another. We highly recommend all couples read the 5 love languages together and take the assessment to identify your own Love Languages. Trust us, it will save you a lot of disagreements and misunderstandings.

Speaking of assessments, we also strongly recommend utilizing a Kolbe R Index.

So, I know some of you may be thinking, how odd it would be to quiz and make your significant other take a "test", right? But listen, you will be so happy you took the few minutes out of your day to take the time to really get to know your love on a much deeper level. So let me just start off by saying that I'm a sucker for a good guide to personality types and behaviors. But The Kolbe R Index is not a personality test. It's a cognitive assessment designed to specifically identify what you are looking for in a personal relationship, based on how you intuitively respond and react to problem solving and conflict. It's great to identify these needs early on so that you can understand your internal expectations and needs from each other. You can find a link to the Love Language quiz and Kolbe R Index at the end of the chapter.

Survival Tip #2: Communicate your Expectations

Hello Readers, I think this is a good place for me to jump in. I'm sure my beautiful wife would agree, this second lesson is something we both had to learn the hard way (especially her, joking but not really).

In an LDR, although you may not be able to immediately determine where you expect it to go, it's pretty clear within the first couple of months whether both parties are committed to the process. It is very important that both participants make it known exactly what their expectations are within the relationship and in what "Reasonable" time frame. Now with that said, if you are expecting your significant other to move, get married and produce kids within the first few months of your relationship...that's what I would call "Un"-Reasonable in which I would reasonably tell you to RUN! Now with that said, if a decent amount of time has gone by and you see a future, there has to be a time that you communicate what you want.

After a year of dating, my now wife made it VERY clear, "She did not want to continue in a long-distance relationship forever." In all fairness, I did not either, but her timeframe and mine did not match. Although she vocalized what she did not want, which she's good at I might add, there was no mention of what she actually DID want specifically. For instance, I had no idea she wanted us to be in the same city by 2016 (smh). Or even that she had a predetermined wedding date, venue, bridesmaid and guest list, seating arrangements, and reception dance all orchestrated and planned out in her mind. Furthermore, come to find out, all of this had already been vocalized to her friends and family. Yes, evidently, I was the last to know.

She didn't communicate her expectations! From my perspective, we were having the best time and starting to get in a nice flow. Her mounting displeasure regarding our current living situation was pretty ridiculous since in my mind we had "just" got back together.

Secondly, it's important to understand our expectations are typically going to be a bit more.....shall I say "measured?" Meaning, we tend to be a little more cautious with regard to our view of how fast or slow a relationship is supposed to go. This is exactly why everything comes back to COMMUNICATION. I would even go as far as to say over-communication is actually a good thing. Once we figured out how to effectively communicate our expectations, it actually brought us closer together because we were no longer playing the guessing game.

Survival Tip#3: Communicate in Person, not just over the Phone

Have you ever found yourself saying, " Let's not talk about that right now, we only have a little time together, let's just enjoy it." One of the common mistakes of LDR couples is that we are so wrapped up in trying to enjoy the time we have in-person that we avoid the uncomfortable conversations to avoid messing up the long weekend we have planned. It creates a false fairy tale and unrealistic perception of what a relationship really is. Although it may make for an uncomfortable minute or two, we still have to create a habit of using the time we have together in person to also tackle those not-so-fun topics to build a healthy long-lasting relationship. Concerned about something your significant other does or does not do? Say it. Want to expound upon the argument you had over the phone where you didn't feel satisfied with the outcome? Talk about it. If you don't, when you do finally live in the same city or house, you will have built a horrible habit of not confronting issues that will ultimately devastate and possibly end your relationship. When Taurean and I made this realization, we began to settle whatever issue we had head-on when we were together. This allowed us to quickly move past obstacles and not harbor bad feelings or hold things in and internalize over them.

Survival Tip #4 Ask more questions that allow you to get to know each other better

In my open letter, you read my mention of Vulnerability and it being the key to making a deep connection. Just in case you missed it, let me repeat it for the fellas in the back lol, "The key to making a deep connection is VULNERABILITY". It definitely took time for me to fully understand the process of how vulnerability leads to a strong human connection, and a strong connection leads to intimacy. Now, for some, the first thing you may think of is physical intimacy (especially with us men lol), but that is not what I'm talking about. It is rather the emotional aspect of intimacy that creates the most intensity. Many are hesitant to allow ourselves to be vulnerable due to our fears. Our human nature is to only open up about what we perceive to be acceptable by someone else's standards, instead of having the willingness to expose our full identity. Fear tends to play a role in stopping us from truly allowing another person in to get to know our true self, but we must remember that emotional intimacy derived from vulnerability is vital to any long-lasting healthy relationship.

There are several studies that show vulnerability forces us to be closer to the individuals we disclose our most intimate desires and thoughts with. It is a human tendency to avoid topics or things that can have us feeling uncomfortable or awkward. Surveys from successful couples show that when we allow ourselves to be transparent and vulnerable about our thoughts and identities, we have a far greater chance of sustaining a healthy relationship.

In our preparation for writing this book, we came across a study that believes that certain questions can be used to accelerate intimacy between a couple.

Below are the 36 Questions used in the study:
*Link to study can be found at the end of this chapter
Set I

1. Given the choice of anyone in the world, whom would you want as a dinner guest?
2. Would you like to be famous? In what way?
3. Before making a telephone call, do you ever rehearse what you are going to say? Why?
4. What would constitute a "perfect" day for you?
5. When did you last sing to yourself? To someone else?
6. If you were able to live to the age of 90 and retain either the mind or body of a 30-year-old for the last 60 years of your life, which would you want?
7. Do you have a secret hunch about how you will die?
8. Name three things you and your partner appear to have in common.
9. For what in your life do you feel most grateful?
10. If you could change anything about the way you were raised, what would it be?

11. Take four minutes and tell your partner your life story in as much detail as possible.

12. If you could wake up tomorrow having gained any one quality or ability, what would it be?

Set II

13. If a crystal ball could tell you the truth about yourself, your life, the future, or anything else, what would you want to know?

14. Is there something that you've dreamed of doing for a long time? Why haven't you done it?

15. What is the greatest accomplishment of your life?

16. What do you value most in a friendship?

17. What is your most treasured memory?

18. What is your most terrible memory?

19. If you knew that in one year you would die suddenly, would you change anything about the way you are now living? Why?

20. What does friendship mean to you?

21. What roles do love and affection play in your life?

22. Alternate sharing something you consider a positive characteristic of your partner. Share a total of five items.

23. How close and warm is your family? Do you feel your childhood was happier than most other people's?

24. How do you feel about your relationship with your mother?

Set III

25. Make three true "we" statements each. For instance, "We are both in this room feeling ... "

26. Complete this sentence: "I wish I had someone with whom I could share ... "

27. If you were going to become a close friend with your partner, please share what would be important for him or her to know.

28. Tell your partner what you like about them; be very honest this time, saying things that you might not say to someone you've just met.

29. Share with your partner an embarrassing moment in your life.

30. When did you last cry in front of another person? By yourself?
31. Tell your partner something that you like about them already.
32. What, if anything, is too serious to be joked about?

Survival Tip #5 Learn how to Resolve Conflict

The art of resolving conflicts in a relationship is not a skill perfected overnight. As a couple, we had to lean on a lot of research and experiences of others to really get to a place where we could both utilize techniques to de-escalate heated arguments. Below, we've included some tips from what we learned from a great source on how to resolve conflicts.

Disagreements obviously mean differences of opinions are present, the plus side of that is, at least there's an indication that you both are willing to express what you think and feel. Many associate conflict as a bad thing but mastering the art of resolving it is a sign of growth and maturity.

Here's some key takeaways we've used throughout our Journey:

1. **Create a welcoming environment for open communication.**
   In a healthy relationship, you and your partner can communicate openly about what is bothering you and what is going well in the relationship. It's important to not only talk about the problems in the relationship but also the positives so no one feels like they are doing everything wrong. If you feel like you can't talk openly about important things, like life issues, money, aspirations, and anything big picture that scares or matters to you, then that is a sign that your relationship may be unhealthy. If you can't express your feelings without fear of retaliation from your partner or them getting overly upset and defensive, then you may be in an abusive relationship.
2. **Maintain a calm and respectful demeanor during heated conversations.**
   Don't cross lines and start insulting your partner. Keep the focus

of the dispute on the issue at hand and don't bring personal jibes and put-downs into it. Also, if your partner consistently gets very heated, aggressive or starts cursing, then those are signs that your relationship may be abusive. No matter what caused the argument, no one should yell at you, curse, or otherwise make you feel uncomfortable and/or scared when you are arguing. You should never feel like you are being attacked or need to tread carefully to not make your partner any angrier.

3. **Get to the root of the problem.**

Sometimes when you argue with your partner it is because someone's needs are not being met. If it seems like your partner is sweating the small stuff, take a moment to evaluate whether there is a larger issue at hand. For instance, if your partner is upset that you are partying in the middle of the week, they might want you to designate more time for your relationship or be worried about you keeping your grades up. Consider things from your partner's point of view and put yourself in their shoes – how would you feel if the roles were reversed? Be understanding of your partner instead of just trying to push your point across.

4. **Watch out for arguments that stem from a need for control.**

If you feel like your partner may be trying to control what you do, then that is a BIG red flag. If your partner is mad that you text other people, doesn't like you prioritizing school and responsibilities over them, pressures you to hook up with them, or tries to limit the time you spend with friends, then those are signs that your partner may be trying to control you. Even if they try to rationalize it by saying they "I'm just over-protective," "it's my trust issues," or it's "because I love you," no one should ever try to control you, especially not your partner. If any of these behaviors sound familiar, your relationship may be abusive and you should seek help.

5. **Find some middle-ground.**

Finding a balance between what both partners want and are comfortable with is very important. If you both care about making the relationship work you will come to an agreement on things without feeling like you are making huge sacrifices for your relationship. Compromising is a key way to resolve conflicts, and finding a middle-ground might be easier than you think! If you are arguing about spending time with your friends or your partner's friends, alternate days to spend time with each friend group or do your own thing for a night. If you feel like your partner is always eating all of your food, ask them to chip in the next time you go grocery shopping.

6. **Agree to disagree and choose your battles.**
Sometimes we need to consider whether what we are fighting about is really worth arguing over. Is it just a matter of what to eat for dinner? Sharing the covers? What should your next Netflix binge be? If the problem is small, sometimes it's best to just drop it. If you won't be mad about it next week, then it's probably not worth your energy. You won't agree with your partner on absolutely everything, and if you feel like the issue is too big to drop then you should contemplate if you and your partner are really compatible.

7. **Consider if the issue is resolvable or not.**

Sometimes we argue with our partner about something that is REALLY big and impacts our lives – like transferring schools, if you do or don't want kids, and where to live when you graduate. If you feel like you will need to sacrifice your beliefs, morals, or dreams to make the relationship work, then you should think about whether this relationship is really worth staying in. For a relationship to succeed, you and your partner should see eye-to-eye on the bigger picture. Having aligned goals, dreams, values, and beliefs is a major part of being compatible with someone.

Source:

https://www.joinonelove.org/learn/handling_conflict/

Communication, Do's, Don'ts, Definitely's:
Do: Set Expectations and Timeline
Don't: Hold in talking about important things in person just make the best out of the "little" time you have together
Definitely: Be willing to "over" communicate, it really is the key to a strong lasting relationship

Resources:

5 Love Languages Quiz: https://www.5lovelanguages.com/profile/couples/

Kolbe R Index: https://www.kolbe.com/?kap-code=A3AF4A0A30574C36A5D78E9D5B33764C&entry_redirect=4

Chapter Three: Those without a Plan, Plan to Fail

Obviously, the majority of the time spent in an LDR is by phone. There are many obstacles such as full-time jobs, businesses, school, kids, and family that impact time spent together. With that said, making sure to spend quality time with your love-one can be pretty challenging at times. We realized pretty quickly that if we didn't actually calendar our virtual date nights, we would literally never see each other. It became very clear we needed to create a plan. This led to us agreeing on a few non-negotiables. The first one was that we spoke with each other every night before bed, and every morning no matter what. For some couples, I'm sure there will be exceptions to this rule (Military couples, couples in different countries, financial limitations) so I would adjust this rule to fit your situation. We also identified things the other liked to do, so we could add more opportunities to do things together. Taurean loved playing fantasy football, so guess what? I played fantasy football too. Even to this day we really enjoy playing against each other within the same leagues. I'm a big movie lover, so we would plan movie dates via Netflix or other on-demand platforms and watch together on Face-Time. All of our favorite tv shows were recorded and our standing rule was not to watch until we could schedule a time to do so together. We recommended certain books or podcasts to each other and looked forward to hearing each other's views or opinions about what we read or listened to. By implementing these small habits, we were intentional about our commitment to spending more quality time with each other. This helped us avoid long gaps in our communication and in turn created more consistency in our relationship.

Survival Tip #6: Know when you plan to see each other In-Person and Commit to It

Another important aspect of our dating plan was to know exactly when we were going to see each other in person again. What worked for us was creating a rotation schedule where I would fly to California every other month and Taurean to Houston every other month. This way we knew exactly when we would see each other. We know for sure flights between California and Texas were definitely not cheap, so if flying every other month is not in your budget, at least have a solid idea of when you will see each other next. For us just knowing that we were going to see each other again on a specific date made leaving each other much easier to digest. It was like we had something to look forward to, which made the dreaded LDR waiting period between in-person visits, much more bearable.

Survival Tip #7: Plan vacations outside of your own City's

After traveling back and forth from Texas to California, we started to notice a dull trend. In my city we would do the same thing over and over; movie, bar, chill at the house, and in his city we would repeat the same cycle. To keep our bi-coastal relationship spontaneous, we got out of the comfort of each of our own homes and planned trips to other places like Mexico, Puerto Rico, Las Vegas, Los Angeles, etc. It gave us a change of scenario and we both were on neutral ground to really genuinely be focused on each other instead of our home routines.

Survival Tip #8: Plan your Personal/Social Time

I know it can be easy to not want to go out or hang with friends when you are in an LDR because you would much rather sit at home on the phone with your love. But resist the urge to do that every day or all weekend. It is important to not lose your own identity. Let your partner know (in advance) that one Friday night during the month, that you will have to reschedule a date night to go hang with the girls and vice versa for the fellas. It's ok, to still have a personal life and do things independently from your significant other in an LDR. It's actually more important than you think. Let's just be honest, no one wants to be with a super "needy" partner. And eventually being overly absorbed in your relationship without outside outlets can become somewhat of a burden to the opposite partner. The healthiest relationships have a balance of individuality and commonality, meaning both parties obviously overlap their activities and similarities but also acknowledge and support their partner's individual lives and activities, and respect their time alone or with other people.

Just like it's important to have some "Me" time in any Non-LDR relationship it's just as important to have "me" time within an LDR relationship. Studies show that setting aside time with your friends has many benefits such as increasing productivity and happiness. Spending time with your friends can also provide models of healthy relationships that you can discuss with your partner/spouse to apply to your relationship. To this point it's perfectly fine to designate some time with your boys or girls for a fun night out, it's actually essential that you do.

Make Your Plan, Do's, Don'ts, Definitely's:

Do: Create opportunities to spend quality time other than just sitting on the phone

Don't: Fall into the trap of doing the same things over and over

Definitely: Mix it up! Plan trips together in neutral places.

Chapter Four: Love is great but Trust is better

Relationships are hard on their own but an LDR can be voluntary torture. The #1 reason LDR's don't work is because of trust. When we decided to restart our relationship in 2014, we dealt with overcoming a lot of trust issues. It's no secret to our friends and family that our first go-round was overshadowed by infidelity and serious immaturity. We both reflect back on that time and cringe, but before moving forward we had to really take a deep dive to identify where we went wrong. We had to make a conscious decision to forgive each other for our mistakes but also dedicate ourselves to doing whatever it took to build back confidence in each other. We first had to start with being vulnerable and accepting, acknowledging and owning the role we individually played to cause the breakdown. I'm certain some of you definitely don't need us to tell you but it's super important that if both parties of the relationship are committed to making it work, that they keep trust as the #1 priority. This, in a lot of ways, is the foundation of any relationship. Whether it's a close friendship, non-LDR relationship, business partnership, or family relationship, you have to maintain trust at all times.

Survival Tip #8: Know your partner's schedule, and make sure they know yours

Ok, remember when Taurean recommended "OVER" communicating? Well, this is one of those times when it's super important in an LDR and honestly in any type of relationship. Let's imagine that you are planning to take your mom to brunch on Sunday, or already scheduled to meet up with the fellas on Thursday for a few pickup games. These are things that you should communicate and make your partner aware of. One of the things that Taurean and I got a lot better at, was communicating what our plans were days, weeks, or even months in advance. This way, you know ahead of time each other's time obligations and can sync your schedules so that you're both doing outside things at the same time, which means more quality time together.

Survival Tip#9: No new friends of the opposite sex

This is probably a section I should let my lovely wife narrate but to the fella's, man to man, Don't Do It! As innocent as it always is, somehow it has a way of becoming a problem that was never intended. Keep the Sara's, Jessica's, Tiffany's, and Ebony's strictly professional. As in if they aren't a part of your 9-5 work curriculum it's probably best to avoid these interactions. It only causes confusion and insecurity down the road. Now, this rule more than likely applies across the board whether it's a normal or LDR relationship but this becomes even more heightened when there's distance involved. Just play it smart and avoid it if at all possible.

Seriously, the "the no new friends rule" applies to the fellas AND the ladies. Secretly, I always believed the rapper Drake was referring to LDR's when he created the hit song. Honestly, it doesn't matter how secure you are in your relationship, when you add distance to the equation, sometimes just the unknown can cause you to second guess yourself and your partner. Introducing a new "friendship" during your time apart from each other could be very intimidating. Just imagine, someone else getting the time that you so desperately want but can't have due to distance, or you not being able to meet someone in person to get a good feel for their intentions with your significant other. As time matures your relationship, your partner should become your best friend, your confidant, your support system and everything in between.

Survival Tip#10: The Jealousy Giant

Ok ladies, so unfortunately I have to admit, that I have shown a small touch of jealousy here and there (I'm sure my husband would disagree with me using the word "small"). And trust me it's never a pretty accessory, and may or may not end you up in jail (That's another book too..lol just "kidding"). At the end of the day, jealousy is one of the most unbecoming characteristics of a person not to mention extremely unhealthy. It's unfair to make your partner suffer through constantly having to affirm their commitment and trustworthiness and honestly it's exhausting. I'm speaking to the women now; from personal experience, I know how hard it is to just "get over it" after your trust has been betrayed. It's not like you magically get a barrel full of trust juice that is overflowing and never-ending. With that said, at the end of the day IF(and I mean a big IF) you decide to be in a relationship after some form of broken trust, you have to start with a clean new slate. One that isn't attached to the past. With Trust, there is no jealousy, because you believe in your partner's commitment to honor you and only act in the best interest of your relationship.

Trust, Do's, Don'ts, Definitely's:

Do: Share your schedule and other important tasks and timelines of your life with your significant other, communicate when there are unexpected changes

Don't: Keep secrets or try to hide things even if you want to protect your significant other

Definitely: Be completely honest and transparent about EVERYTHING

Chapter Five: K.I.S.S.- Keep it Spicy & Sexy

So let me start this chapter by pointing out that although Taurean and I made a conscious decision to have premarital sex before getting married, I believe that we endured far more issues within our relationship that could have possibly been avoided if we had abstained. As a Believer, looking back, I wish once we decided to get back together we would have taken some time to have a serious conversation about abstinence. We by no means are condoning any preference, condemning, or judging anyone's choices but more so want to share our experience as honestly and transparently as possible. With that being said, sex or no sex, we both believe that intimacy and attraction energy is very important in a relationship. And within an LDR sometimes you have to be creative because the organic escalation of intimacy that happens in a normal distance relationship can be harder to keep. So, over the 4 years, we spent in two different states, there were several things we did to keep it alive and fresh.

So now that we have the disclaimer out of the way (wink wink) let me jump in to state the obvious; an LDR definitely presents some challenges when it comes to maintaining some type of intimacy. Now I'd love to tell you how I would surprise Shauna with surprise romantic gestures like, coming down her street on a white horse with a chef and picnic table awaiting us under a clear sunset, but the truth is I just was not that creative. Spontaneous yes, but I guess I didn't read enough romance novels to spark the creative gene when it came to those ideas. With that said, we still created fun and romantic moments throughout our LDR tenure. What I learned is that it's the simple things women really appreciate like sending flowers randomly or writing a handwritten letter expressing your feelings or even sending surprise gifts from time to time.

Survival Tip #11: Have Fun!

Not being in the same city, has a way of expunging every ounce of your creativity. After about the first year of being in an LDR, we learned to find unique ways to keep things fun and interesting. Here's a list of our favorites:

1. Learn Something New Together
2. Play Games Online; (One of us is terrible at Chess, but the other stills like to gloat when they win) We also recommend a fun virtual experience with, Let's Roam. Find some fun things at http://www.letsroam.com/sdcvision
3. Take turns being a DJ and play each other some of your favorite songs
4. Create a vision board of the things you want to accomplish, experience, or do together and place them somewhere you both can look at them
5. Use the app Scener to have a virtual movie night together
6. Cook dinner together via video chat
7. Plan a destination date
8. Come up with a list of questions to ask each other
9. Start a book club between the two of you
10. Surprise him/her with a round of drinks while their out with their friends to let them know you're thinking of them

These are just a couple of recommendations we mixed in during our time apart. The key is to find ways to stay connected.

K.I.S.S., Do's, Don'ts, Definitely's:

Do: Openly discuss what things you like when it comes to intimacy and affection

Don't: Get sucked into the mundane routine and forget to have intimacy and spice in person and not

Definitely: Get creative and get outside of your comfort zone

Chapter Six: For Long Distance Couples w/Children

This chapter is for couples that have children outside of the relationship. We should probably call this a section as opposed to a chapter because to be honest, we DID NOT do our best to make sure our children were well acclimated to each other before getting married and therefore are offering recommendations based on what we "Wish" we would have done. On the other hand, that's exactly why we wanted to include this "section", for the many parents out there like us who will wish someone told them. When we decided to recommit we both had two boys from previous relationships. We really underestimated what obstacles we would face while trying to blend our families. We strongly recommend if you have children, have both decided you are committed to the relationship and some time has gone by, start finding ways to integrate your children into the relationship and to each other, if both parties are parents.

After doing some research, here are some ideas on how to introduce your child/children to your significant other and potential siblings:

1. **In the beginning, have low Expectations:**
   Introducing a child to a new love interest could be intimidating, especially if the child has aspirations for their parents to get back together. When the relationship is at a point that you're both ready to make an introduction to a new significant other, make sure you're not expecting too much from either your child or your new partner and that it's a low-stress meeting. You can even consider making it very casual and brief.

2. **Slowly start building a Relationship:**

   If children are old enough to have phones, include them in a group chat with parent and significant other. Regularly send a funny or loving text. If younger children send fun cards or small gifts in the mail.

3. **Include them in Calls regularly:**

   In a long-distance relationship, more than likely you have some scheduled times to talk to your significant other. Have another schedule to speak to the child, or even call just to speak to them only sometimes.

4. **Pay attention to their interest and genuinely listen when you talk:**

Children have a sixth sense for pretend and disingenuous attention. If you are serious

about your relationship and its potential to result in marriage, a healthy loving

connection with children outside the relationship is extremely important.

Long-Distance Parenting, Do's, Don'ts, Definitely's:

Do: Intentionally include children in the communication schedule to build a relationship

Don't: Force a fake relationship and get aggravated with children if there is some push back

Definitely: Stay committed and consistent to grow a healthy, loving bond

Chapter Seven: Manifest Your Mate

I really do attest my belief in "manifesting a mate" to a good friend of mine that I once saw on Facebook, describing a "Date Night" with her husband. I later found out that this same friend was not only, NOT married but was also not even dating anyone at the time. After talking to her a little more, she shared with me that, one day she just made a decision that she desired a husband and knew exactly how to attract her heart's desire. What was her secret? The powerful use of her words and thoughts. She immediately began the habit of publicly talking about her husband and all the things that they did together as if they were already happening. She would post about date nights and things he would say to make her laugh. And if you didn't know her personally, you were totally convinced that she and her "husband" were the happiest couple. Day after day she practiced affirming and professing. And guess what!? Not shortly after harnessing the power of belief, she fell in love with the man of her dreams and sailed happily into matrimonial bliss. Sounds a little crazy huh? I thought so too, lol. But as I became growingly frustrated from repeated failed relationships, I started to ask myself what exactly did I have to lose. It was about one year into Taurean and my long-distance relationship when I began to realize the many differences we had. As he mentioned at the beginning of the book he dealt with having to overcome a lot of immaturities and honestly he was not alone. We both had to grow individually and as a couple. Although we both were committed to the relationship there were a lot of gaps and missing elements that would allow us to sustain a healthy relationship. I was not at all happy with how Taurean communicated, his lack of sympathy or sincerity. His insensitivity and his lack of vulnerability and transparency. He was everything I wanted on the outside, but my heart yearned for a different man on the inside. It was during this time of questioning if I was with the right person or not, that I was reminded of my friend on Facebook. And I decided to be more intentional about what I wanted and adopted my own manifesting routine that I'd love to share with you. I Like to call this routine, the 3 Must do's to Manifest Your Mate.

1. Define the Desire
2. "Write the Vision, Make it Plain"
3. Vision Immersion

1. DEFINE your Desires: What exactly do you want in a mate? Now, before you answer that question, let me let you in on a little secret. Defining what you want in a mate, should not have anything to do with a person's physical attributes and neither their financial nor material means. When considering what you desire, think about characteristics that impact how you "feel", emotionally and spiritually.

Before I began to be intentional about my words and thoughts in regard to attracting the mate that I desired, I had to first define what that was. After many weeks of evaluating myself and past experiences, I was clear on what God qualities I wanted in a man that would align with my beliefs and love languages.

2. WRITE your Desires: Writing down your desires is an underused extreme superpower that we all have. Written desires are a strong visual reminder and leave a powerful imprint on the mind, which ultimately transform themselves into physical beings and things. By writing your desires down, your brain is more likely to receive, believe and attract exactly what you have written. Seeing your desires on paper triggers your brain to create an emotional attachment, which is where the true magic happens. I personally used these principles and began to write down my desires religiously, 3 times a day. I carried a small pocket journal everywhere I went for 3 years, and even set an alarm with my own voice to remind me to continue to write it down. Through this process,

I personally experienced the power of true manifestation. All the things that I wrote and prayed daily for in a mate, came to life. Many understand the power of speaking your desires or affirmations but the alignment of speaking your desires, with writing them consistently, expedites the results, compared to just saying them out loud.

3. IMMERSE yourself in the Vision: There are scientific studies that show the most effective way to learn, adapt or fuse yourself to something new, is to immerse yourself into it. If you want to learn French, the quickest way to learn is to move to France. If you want to learn to swim, you have to get into the water. Webster's definition of Immersion is "deep mental involvement". As I mentioned earlier, the mind has to make an emotional attachment to your desires to align those desires with God and your belief system. So how do you immerse yourself to cause an emotional attachment? You do exactly what my friend from Facebook and I did. You talk and act as if what you want is already a reality. I love how when you start seeking a particular thing it returns the favor and reaches out to find you. At a time when I started to apply these principles to my daily routine, my aunt recommended a book that changed my life, so I will now recommend it to you. It's called the Power of a Praying Wife by Stormie Omartian (There is also a Power of a Praying Husband for my fellas) Purchase your copies here, under "Books and Digital Downloads" http://www.amazon.com/shop/shaunadcurry

Because my desires included being a wife, I started praying for my husband years before I was even engaged. This book helped me align my desires into specific prayers and create that emotional connection needed to build the characteristics and heart of what I wanted in a mate. Daily I made it a practice to pray for my husband before I knew who he was and God moved to make my prayers a reality. Every whispered prayer was answered in my now lifelong partner.

In addition to preparing as a wife, when it came to manifesting my mate, I took my belief to the next level and picked a wedding date and put it on all my friend's calendars. Not only did I pick a date, but I also started to plan the wedding, and yes, all before ever being engaged or even being sure that I was in the right relationship. You see, it is not our job to figure out how things will work out, our job is only to believe and trust the principles of power God gave each and every one of us.

Here are some Key Takeaways;

1. Get the book
2. Write Daily, multiple times a day if possible
3. Speak, act, and believe to the point people think you're crazy

Manifest Your Mate, Do's, Don'ts, Definitely's:
Do: Identify your Desires
Don't: Stop being consistent with your writing, and immersion
Definitely: Believe, get emotionally attached, and Expect it is done!

Chapter Eight: The Proposal

Ah, the proposal. Well, it happened, but not really how I envisioned it to play out. We've all seen the countless proposals on social media and TV. The man takes the lady to dinner at one of her favorite restaurants, a sentimental location or even a meaningful first-date venue that has some type of nostalgia. Her friends and family pop up out of nowhere to witness the occasion, and so on. All seemingly very romantic right? Well, our proposal didn't check any of those boxes. It kind of just happened, all while in a Mexican bathroom, but hey, at least it was a nice bathroom. Let me explain.

A few months before the summer of 2018 Shauna and I decided to plan a trip to Cabo San Lucas, Mexico. We were super excited but leading up to the trip I could feel we were hitting a relationship resistance level. I could sense she was getting tired of the boyfriend/girlfriend status and wanted more. Not that I didn't as well, it was just my timeline was lagging a bit behind hers, although I knew in my gut it was time.

As the date drew closer for our trip, I began to contemplate making this the moment to pop the question. The timing made sense logically so I started to do my research on rings; I already knew her ring size and had an idea of what she would like. After a few weeks of ring hunting in California and not finding what I was looking for I reached out to a good friend of hers who connected me with a ring specialist, she knew in Houston. After speaking with her we agreed to meet the next time I was in town. A few days before our scheduled departure to Mexico I flew out to Houston and luckily was able to find a ring I felt she'd be proud to wear.

Fast forward to travel day, all I could think about was, where do I hide the ring? At what juncture of the trip do I propose? How do I propose? What if a TSA rep pulls it out of my luggage during the security check right in front of her? As life would have it, this question was about to be answered. After coming out of the body scanner I saw my bag in slow motion begin to take the "alternate route of doom" on the baggage carousel. My armpits began to sweat profusely as the TSA rep uttered "whose bag is this?". "Mine," I whispered in hopes no one else would hear me but him.

As he began to open my bag to initiate the search, I surveyed the scene to see where Shauna was located. It didn't take long to realize she was standing right beside me, staring back at me crazy, as if she couldn't wait to tell me how much of an amateur packer I was. As he began to unzip the small pocket zipper, I felt as if I was shooting a signature double-dolly scene from a Spike Lee film; the ones where the main character floats towards their destruction.

He began to pull out a few things one item at a time. Right before he began to raise his arm to pull out another item I saw what seemed to be a bit of hesitation. He looked up at me and I looked directly at him as if we were in a country-western showdown. The stare felt like it lasted for 5 long minutes. I was hoping he could recognize the look on my face as a desperate plea for help. Typically in these types of uneasy situations, I could always think of something, but at this moment the only thing that came to mind was if he pulled the ring out, to just take a knee and propose right there on the spot, barefoot and all. After breaking eye contact he began to smile, took his empty hand out of my bag, gave me the "nod" and sent me on my way. Shauna had no idea how close she was to being proposed to at Terminal C of Hobby Airport right before our trip even began.

As I got on the plane and sat down I belted out a sigh of relief but the hard part was still to come. When do I actually propose? You can probably tell by now I wasn't much of a planner, so the thought of this was admittedly nerve-wracking.

Finally settled in Mexico, Day 1 didn't seem like the right time to propose. It was early evening by the time we arrived at the resort and once we unpacked and got settled, we decided to relax at the pool, eat something quick, and relax in the room the rest of the night watching Netflix.

On Day 2 we wanted to do something fun and adventurous so we went ziplining and ATV riding. Unbeknownst to us there were 10 different ziplines on the course we chose. Each one consisted of us having to walk higher and higher up a mountain to a zipline that got longer and longer each time. Being that Shauna was ready to abandon ship after the first one, her fear, frustration and irritability grew after each one. Which in turn caused us to almost break up a few times right before each zipline circuit. Needless to say, it just didn't seem like the right opportunity to ask for her hand in marriage lol.

Day 3 I planned for us to have dinner that night at a really nice steak restaurant that overlooked the ocean in the mountains of the resort. I remember having the ring in my pocket the entire day leading up to dinner just in case the perfect moment transpired. Well it didn't, but I knew dinner was to come. Shauna looked amazing as we walked out of our room to the restaurant. The entire time on our way to eat I told myself it's now or never, there's no better time than now.

As we waited within the lounge area to be seated, the butterflies began to flutter within me. I don't think I spoke much at all while we waited to be seated. As the night wore on after being seated and ordering our entrees, I knew showtime was drawing nearer. You could hear the sound of the waves bouncing against the walls of the cliffs and the full moon was shining down what felt like right on us. It was an amazing view looking out into the ocean from a 45ft elevation. I must have checked my pocket 100 times by this point to make sure the ring was still there.

When I finally decided the time was right I couldn't help but think should I do this now? Is it too predictable? Should I wait until we go out after dinner? My over-analytical brain got me again and we finished dinner with the ring still left in my pocket, but I thought I now had a plan. I remember there being an area in the middle downtown where I could propose in front of everyone. At this point I had to make it happen, I had no choice, it was now or truly never because we were leaving the next day. The only problem was when we got back to the room after dinner we somehow never made it back out.

As the sun rose on Day 4 I remember waking up in panic mode, feeling like I failed the mission. We were scheduled to leave late afternoon, and I felt as if I was pretty much out of options. As our room service set up our breakfast outside on the patio I noticed Shauna was outside by our private pool, on the phone. I couldn't hear what she was saying but by her body language, she seemed to be dejected. As if something was bothering her and I already knew why. At that moment I knew I could not leave Mexico without accomplishing what I intended to do in the first place.

Right before she got off of the phone I figured it would be a good idea to place the ring under her napkin. As soon as she picked the napkin up to place it on her lap or wipe her mouth I planned to get down on one knee, but that never happened. I don't even think she touched the napkin at all that morning. Another missed opportunity.

After breakfast, we started to pack our bags. I could feel the disappointment without her saying a word. The shame I felt at that moment began to increase with each apparel item folded into the suitcase. When I finished packing I realized she was taking longer than expected packing her toiletries. In my mind this was my last shot to make it happen. With the ring in my hand behind my back I turned the corner into the bathroom area with confidence ready to take the ultimate knee. As I walked closer to her I could see she was already visually emotional before she even realized I was behind her. When she turned around, she looked at me and asked, "why are we not engaged? I was hoping when we left Houston we wouldn't return within the same relationship status." Right then and there I fell to my knee bringing my hand around with the ring case opened. She froze in disbelief as tears began to stream down the side of her face. Honestly I don't remember her actually saying yes, in fact I'm not sure she said anything at all as she was so wrapped up in emotion.

By no means was this the fairytale proposal which we laugh about to this day, but it's a moment in time we'll cherish forever. I'll never forget that moment when she agreed to become Mrs. Curry.

Chapter Nine: Helpful LDR Items

Helpful Item #1: What does Research Say?

LDRs are more common than you think. According to longdistancerelationshps.net 14 to 15 million people consider themselves in a long-distance relationship. 3.75 million married couples are in an LDR and 75% of all engaged couples have been (at some point) in a long-distance relationship. Although an LDR isn't ideal, there are some real advantages that come with the territory we can attest to.

- Companion Pass Qualification/Frequent Flyer Miles
- Improved Communication Skills
- Your Relationship is Based on More than the Physical
- Always Having Something to Look Forward To
- Amazing Story to Tell

Other studies point out long-distance relationships may be just as stable or even more stable in some cases than assumed but only if certain conditions are met. One study in particular (Dargie et al, 2015) examined the relationships of 1,142 couples. Surprisingly, they discovered few differences between LDRs and regular relationships. Research found no evidence that LDRs are at all different in the following categories:

- Intimacy
- Communication
- Relationship satisfaction
- Commitment

• Sexual communication or satisfaction

Helpful Item #2: The 5 Love Languages

Words of Affirmation: Verbal compliments, or words of appreciation, are powerful communicators of love. Examples: "I love you", "You look great in that suit", "You're beautiful", etc. Often considered 'Expressed Love'.

1. *Physical Touch*: Offering your partner an intimate connection with you through holding hands, sitting close together, hugs, kissing, etc.
2. *Quality Time*: Giving someone your undivided attention and genuinely being 'together'. This is not to be confused with watching TV together while being on your phones.
3. *Acts of Service*: Doing things you know your spouse would appreciate or things that would make their life easier, i.e.: cooking a meal, setting a table, emptying the dishwasher, vacuuming, changing the baby's diaper, picking up a prescription, etc. is often considered 'Implied Love'.
4. *Gifts*: The gift itself is a symbol of thought that states, "I was thinking about you" or "I remembered you". Generally, buying them a CD of their favorite band or a shirt from a store they love is a nice, personalized way to love your partner

Helpful Item #3:
10 questions that you should ask each other and answer honestly:

1. How often can you realistically plan to visit each other?
2. Are you willing to move to your significant other's city?
3. If yes, what steps will you take to make it happen?
4. Is marriage important to you?

5. What does marriage mean to you?
6. What do you want in a partner?
7. What are your non-negotiables?
8. What's your biggest fear?
9. What are two things I don't know about you?
10. How okay are you with your partner's closeness to others?

CPSIA information can be obtained
at www.ICGtesting.com
Printed in the USA
BVHW040939040122
625439BV00015B/674

9 780578 837321